I Hate Everything.

Matthew DiBenedetti

adamsmedia
Avon, Massachusetts

Published by Adams Media,
a division of F+W Media, Inc.
57 Littlefield Street,
Avon, MA 02322. U.S.A.
www.adamsmedia.com

Interior illustrations and design by Elisabeth Lariviere
Cover design by Frank Rivera and Jessica Faria

ISBN 10: 1-4405-0638-8
ISBN 13: 978-1-4405-0638-3
eISBN 10: 1-4405-0958-1
eISBN 13: 978-1-4405-0958-2

Printed in the United States of America.

10   9   8   7   6   5   4   3   2   1

Library of Congress Cataloging-in-Publication Data

DiBenedetti, Matthew.
I hate everything. / Matthew DiBenedetti.
p. cm.
ISBN 978-1-4405-0638-3
1. Conduct of life—Humor. 2. Pessimism—Humor. 3. Pessimism—Poetry. I. Title.
PN6231.C6142D53 2010
818'.602—dc22
2010029129

This book is available at quantity discounts for bulk purchases. For information, please call 1-800-289-0963.

This is fondly dedicated from the pit of my soul to all those special people who have helped me build this compilation so easily. You know who you are. Thanks for nothing good . . . except for this.

I hate that some people will be upset that my book wasn't dedicated to them. Trust me—you don't want this dedication.

Introduction

This book of "Hate" was compiled for people like me, who have turned to wholehearted pessimism. We weren't always like this. We used to want to believe that there were plenty of things to be happy about every day, things like rainbows, warm cookies, and candy canes. However, life has worn us down. We now can see that the glass has always been half empty, and that there is really so much to hate. Once you accept this truth, it kind of sets you free and you begin to enjoy it. You can openly express yourself and quickly find that you're not alone. So many people love to hate too!

I appreciate that you are one of those people, even though I probably could find things I hate about you . . . but that's all in the fun of it. I hope you enjoy hating everything with me.

I hate that hate is the way so many of us warm our souls.

I hate that I don't have a soul.

I hate that sunrises happen so early.

I hate that sunsets happen so early.

I hate daylight-savings time.

I hate that I have to keep changing my password.

I hate that I have to keep my password written down next to my computer.

new password | ********** |

re-enter password | **********| |

I hate that I always get stuck with the small slice of pizza.

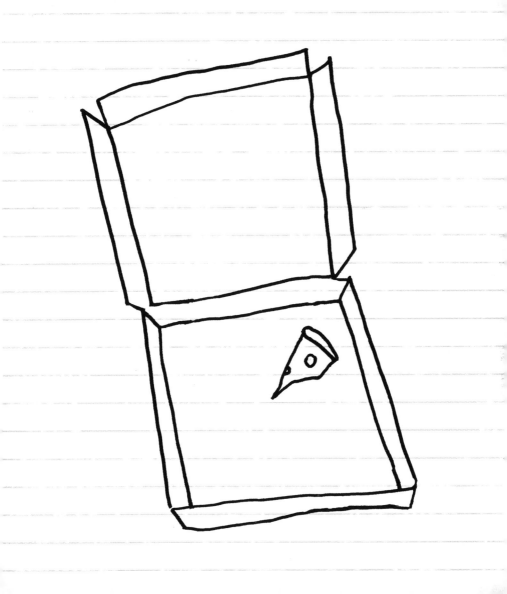

I hate that he has a bigger TV than me.

I hate seeing peanut butter in the jelly jar.

I hate songs that bring back memories.

I hate things that you feel compelled to do annually.

I hate poetry.

I hate finding out that the Easter Bunny doesn't exist.

I hate that now people say Santa doesn't exist either?!

I hate thinking there is a ghost in every
old house.
I hate that there may be a ghost in my house.
I hate that the ghost is always watching me.

I hate thinking that the ghost
is my grandma.

I hate that you only need to exercise for twenty minutes, three times a week to be fit.

I hate that I waste more time than that.

I hate that I'm still not fit.

I hate when people don't embrace change for the better.

I hate change.

I hate the better of two evils.

I really hate the worse of 'em.

I hate waking up on the wrong side of the bed.
I hate when people ask me if I have.
I hate that the snooze button doesn't last longer.

I hate waking up at the witching hour.
I hate drooling in my sleep.
I hate when I don't have my pillow.

I hate when people cramp my space.
I hate that not everyone likes to cuddle.

I hate that breakfast isn't served past 11:00 A.M.
I hate when people eat breakfast for dinner.
I hate when people don't follow rules.
I hate procrastinators.

I hate that mullets went out of style.
I hate people that think they haven't.

I hate the water that magically appears in a mustard bottle.

I hate that it ruins a perfectly good sandwich.

I hate wasting food.

I hate that I'm overweight.

I hate that I have fat clothes.

I hate that I'm wearing my fat clothes.

I hate that I don't get an allowance anymore.
I hate that I still have to take out the trash.

I hate that once you use lip balm, you're hooked for life.

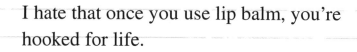

I hate that everything on the Internet isn't true. I hate that the newspaper isn't delivered to the doorstep.

I hate dainty, yappy dogs.

I especially hate their prissy owners.

I hate that I don't have a green thumb.

I hate that plants don't tell me when they are thirsty.

I hate counting down to the New Year.

I hate that it's just another lousy day about to start.

I hate that good food is bad for you.
I hate that manure is used to fertilize
vegetables.
I guess you can understand why . . .

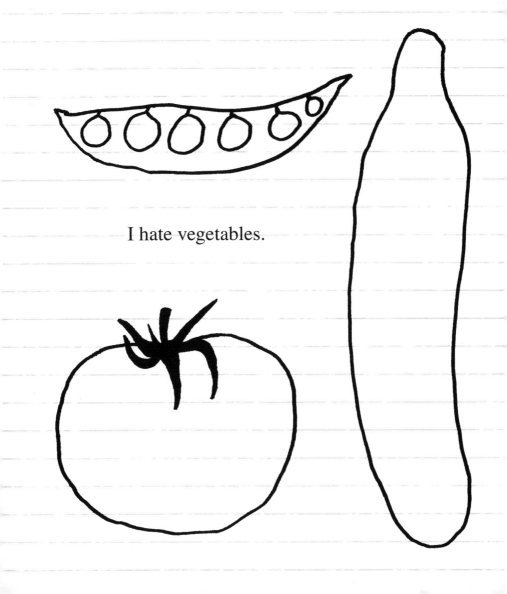

I hate vegetables.

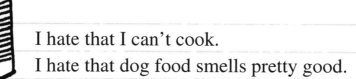

I hate that I can't cook.
I hate that dog food smells pretty good.

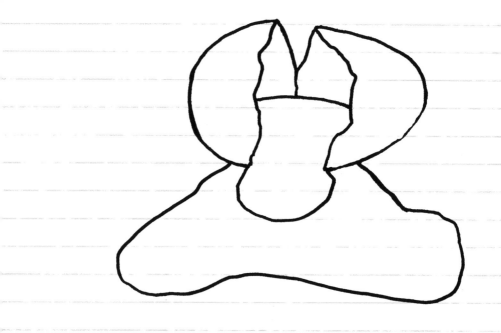

I hate that spell checker isn't always write.

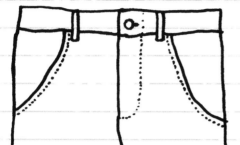

I hate that the corduroy sound isn't louder.

I hate polyester.

I hate that linen wrinkles.

I hate the skin that forms on the top of pudding.

I hate that figgy pudding isn't even pudding at all.

I hate the thought of going bald.

I hate that I still make fun of bald people.
I hate karma.

I hate having low self-esteem.

I hate that coffee doesn't stay hot.
I hate that the cup still says "hot contents" even after it has cooled.
I hate that they have to print that on the side of the cup.
I hate that sugar packets are so small.
I hate that coffee creamer can be nondairy.
I hate coffee breath.

I hate that I need coffee.

I hate that when you pluck a gray hair, three more take its place.

I hate the time I found my first gray hair.

I hate that I named it.

I hate that it has the same name as my ex.

I hate running into exes.
I hate seeing that an ex is clearly doing
well without me.
I hate that I only remember the good times
with my ex.
I hate that the only good times with the ex were
the day we met and the day we broke up.

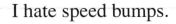

I hate speed bumps.

I hate that I breathe the same air
as everyone else.

I hate that all planes don't skywrite.

I hate dieting.

I hate remote controls that have too many buttons.

I hate that it takes seven remotes to watch one TV.

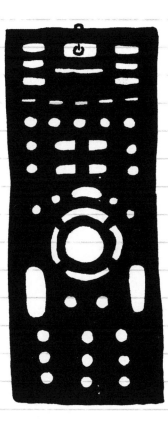

I hate not knowing how to tie a Windsor knot.

I hate clip-on bow ties.

I hate removing Band-Aids.

I hate hairy knuckles.

I hate that they sell pickled pigs feet.

I hate watching movies with people that have
already seen them.
I hate movies that don't have happy endings.
I hate that everything doesn't come with
a happy ending.
I hate that I'm immature enough
to giggle at that.

I hate when leaves fall in my yard.
I hate that my yard doesn't have any trees.

I hate that my neighbors are so close.

I hate when clothes sent to the dry cleaner come back with new stains.

I hate confrontation.

I hate that nervousness makes you sweat.

I hate T-shirt sweat stains.

I hate Mercedes drivers who think they own the road.

I hate that they probably do.

I hate that SUV drivers think they are invincible.

I hate that my SUV isn't invincible.

I hate poor gas mileage.

I hate that sugar tastes so good.

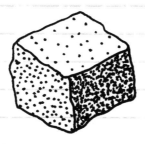

I hate that diet-soda aftertaste.

I hate that all metal isn't heavy.

I hate water that tastes like metal.
I hate when water only dribbles out of public
drinking fountains.
I hate using the lower kiddie drinking fountain.
I hate coming in contact with anything that is
for public use.

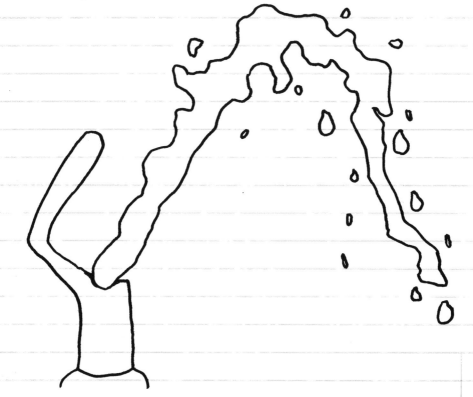

I hate songs sung blue.
I hate that everybody knows one.

I hate that everything isn't always Smurfy.
I hate that Smurfette was the only girl.
I hate that their language actually makes sense.

I hate when it's hard to find the English portion
of an instruction manual.

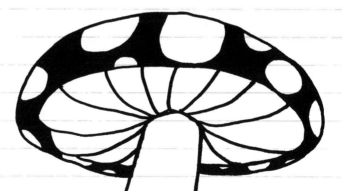

I hate having no patience.

I hate building models.

I hate that puzzles take so long to finish.
I hate that I just want to find one more puzzle
piece before I stop.

I hate wasting time.

I hate typewriters.

I hate that kids today can text faster than I can type.

I hate that I don't have the latest iPhone.

I hate that technology moves so fast.

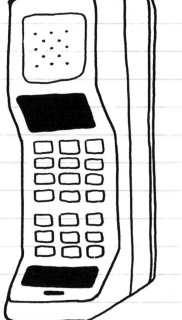

I hate that I thought beta video, laser disk, and HD-DVD would catch on.

I hate having to purchase my favorite movies yet again, to fit my new player.

I hate buying movies that I only watch once.

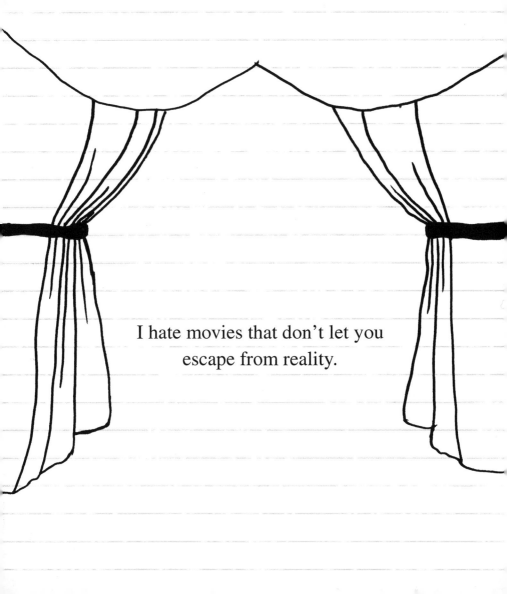

I hate movies that don't let you escape from reality.

I hate tank tops on guys.

I hate that more girls don't wear the Sarah
Connor military-style tank top.
I hate that Sarah Connor can do more pull-ups
than me.

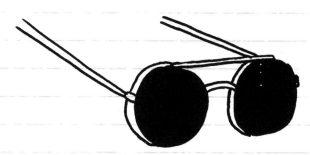

I hate that I'm not the future leader of
the resistance.
I hate that I'll never have a Terminator as
a bodyguard.
I hate that the school bully always said,
"I'll be back."
I hate bullies.

I hate group photos.

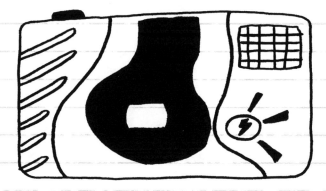

I hate fake smiles.
I hate stale cookies.
I hate when nacho chips get jammed into
your gums.

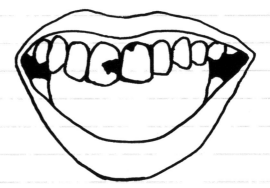

I hate when people don't tell me that I had
something stuck in my teeth.

I hate that my belly button
no longer has a purpose.

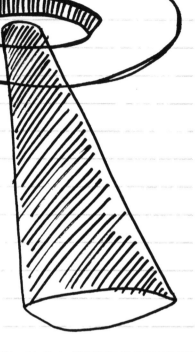

I hate that everyone doesn't migrate south for the winter like geese.

I hate that adding an *s* doesn't make everything plural.

I hate that the people of earth don't use one language.

I hate that movie aliens can speak English.

I hate that nobody has caught the Loch Ness Monster.

I hate big feet.

I hate finding change on the restroom floor.

I hate that I'm too cheap to leave it for someone else.

I hate rest stops.

I hate washing my hands
in a public restroom, then
opening a dirty door.

I hate when fish tastes fishy.
I hate that everything "tastes like chicken."

I hate when people have
birds as pets.

I hate that all pets can't
repeat what they hear.

I hate that my pets fart.

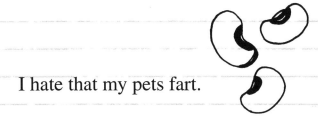

I hate that I can't always blame the pet.

I hate that pets don't outlive humans.

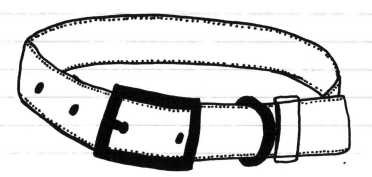

I hate the smell of expired milk.
I hate that milk doesn't last longer.

I hate milk.

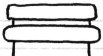

I hate this font.

I hate that every time you open up a book,
it flips to the same page.

I hate that all books aren't on tape.

I hate getting books as gifts.*

*Except this one.

I hate writing Christmas cards.

Happy
Holidays

I hate Christmas picture cards . . . yeah I know,
I haven't seen your family in over a year . . .
and yeah, your kids are still ugly.

I hate that I don't get any Christmas cards.

I hate kitten calendars.

I hate that my skin gets dry in the winter.

I hate when someone asks me to help them lotion their back.

I hate that more things don't come in a tube.

I hate when I forget coupons.

I hate that whenever I pull a number at the deli counter, it's always last.

I hate standing in lines.

I hate that amusement park rides are never worth the long wait.

I hate doing laundry.

I hate when people catch me wearing socks with holes in them.

I hate how socks sag when they are soaking wet.

I hate stepping in a puddle when wearing just socks.

I hate that missing socks are never found.

I hate that major sports teams are named after socks.

I hate that I can't throw a ball.

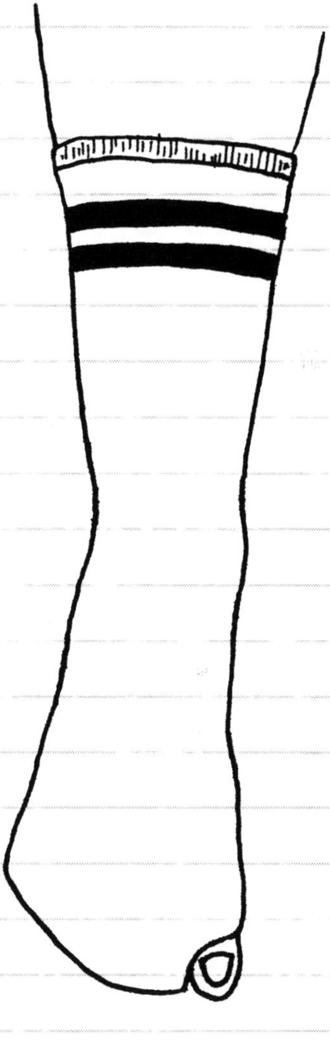

I hate broken crayons.

I hate the color lime green.

I hate that all water isn't Caribbean island blue.

I hate red lights.

I hate brown M&Ms.

I hate that apples brown so quickly.

I hate that stringy stuff down the inside of a banana . . . and, I hate that brown thing at the bottom of a banana.

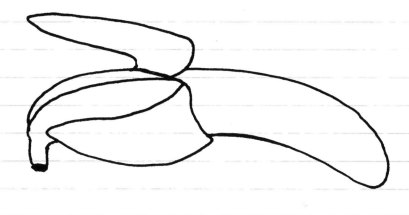

I hate that fruit is so phallic.

I hate testing fruit for freshness at the market.
I hate gutting pumpkins.

I hate that I don't know when to hold 'em or
when to walk away.
I hate that I'm afraid to play craps.
I hate that they call it craps.

I hate that I have crappy luck.

I hate that casinos don't have clocks.
I hate the carpet styles in casinos.
I hate when they implode historic casinos.
I hate that old casinos still exist.

I hate rough towels.
I hate tacky hotel paintings.
I hate that my hotel room is never near the ice machine.
I hate that my hotel room always smells like smoke.
I hate that there are never enough pillows in a hotel room.
I hate hotel pillows.

I hate hard beds.

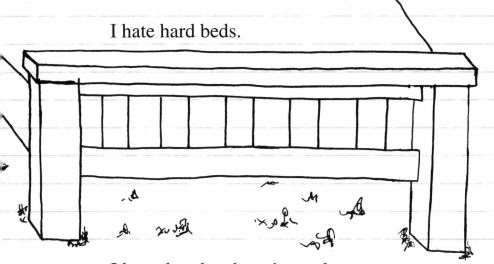

I hate that dust bunnies gather
under my bed.

I hate finding bugs trapped in
my tub.

I hate that lightning bugs don't stay lit.

I hate that the rotary phone went away.
I hate that some people don't even know
what a rotary phone is.

I hate that there are hardly any phone
booths nowadays.

I hate that Superman is running out of places
to change.

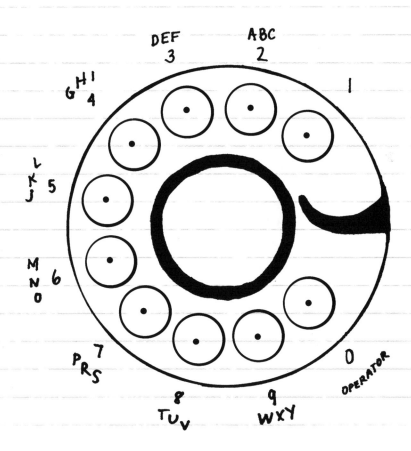

I hate that superheroes
don't really exist.

I hate that villains do.

I hate changing smoke alarm batteries.

I hate changing my flat tire.
I hate changing someone else's flat
even more.
I hate that all cars don't come with a
full-size spare tire.

I hate that my "spare tire" isn't in
my trunk.

I hate that trucks still kick out so much smoky exhaust.

I hate that there are three types of gasoline.

I hate that new sports cars don't rumble like old hot rods.

I hate that it's not encouraged to run idiot drivers off of the road.

I hate trash on the side of the road.

I hate when people ask if my new
outfit was a gift.

I hate that frumpy, comfy flannel
pajamas aren't sexier.

I hate that people think overalls look good.

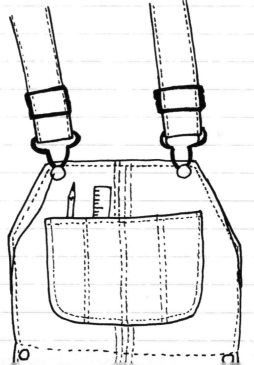

I hate that cut flowers don't last forever.

I hate when people don't light candles because they're "decorative."

I hate scuffing up new shoes.

I hate that we don't use the good china
every day.

I hate that there aren't enough reasons to
use the good china.

I hate that maps have boundaries.

I hate that when I play
"someday I'm going to
live here" on a globe,
I end up in the ocean.

I hate that *Star Wars* was a long, long
time ago . . .
I hate that I will never be able to
own every *Star Wars* action figure.
I hate that Chewbacca's career is
limited to the *Star Wars* movies.
I hate that it took thirty years
to finish the *Star Wars* saga.
I hate that there are only
six episodes.
I hate that I can't growl
like a Wookiee.

I hate that the Force is not strong with me.

I hate auto lease fees.

I hate that the free public library has late fees.
I hate that they probably need that fifteen cents
I had to pay them.

I hate wasting checks for small amounts.

I hate that my checkbook is never balanced.
I hate that it's never in my favor.

758

09/03 20 10

Pay to the order of __Public Library__ $ [0.15]

__fifteen cents__——— Dollars B≡

For __LATE FEE__   _Matthew DiBenedetti_

⑈ ⑈⑈⑈⑈⑈ ⑈⑈ ⑈ ⑈⑈⑈⑈ ⑈⑈ ⑈⑈⑈

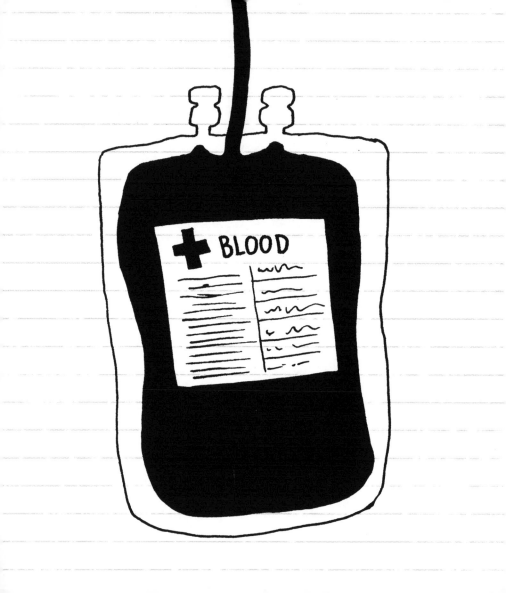

I hate that blood makes me queasy.

I hate that I don't have more blood to donate.

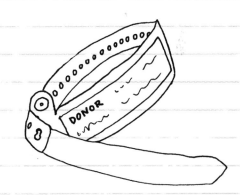

I hate when speakers crack.
I hate when people don't care about their
plumber's crack.

I hate cracking the spine of a new
book; I feel like I'm killing it . . .
like a lobster.

I hate eating a whole fresh lobster.

I hate that those eyes just keep staring at me.

I hate the green, gooey slop inside.

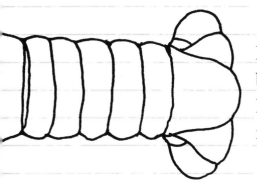

I hate that I love melted butter.
I hate that I can't believe it's not butter.

I hate feeling obligated to look at
peoples' photo albums.

I hate empty liquor bottles.

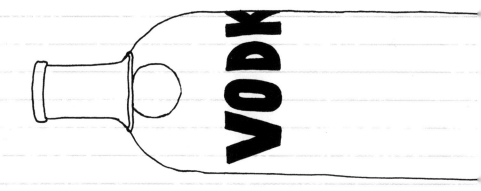

I hate warm beer.
I hate wasting beer.

I hate singing "Happy Birthday."
I hate that you have to let kids blow out
your birthday candles.
I hate that they have more birthdays left
than I do.

I hate that it's bad luck to whistle inside the house (whistling may be one of the only things I mildly enjoy, dammit).

I hate superstitions.

I hate that there isn't always cold pizza
in the fridge.

I hate that my mailbox is on
the curb.

I hate laziness.

I hate that I'm well past puberty and
still get zits.

I hate facial hair.
I hate shaving.
I hate that laser hair removal
costs so much.

I hate my family genes.

I hate living with someone.

I hate being alone.

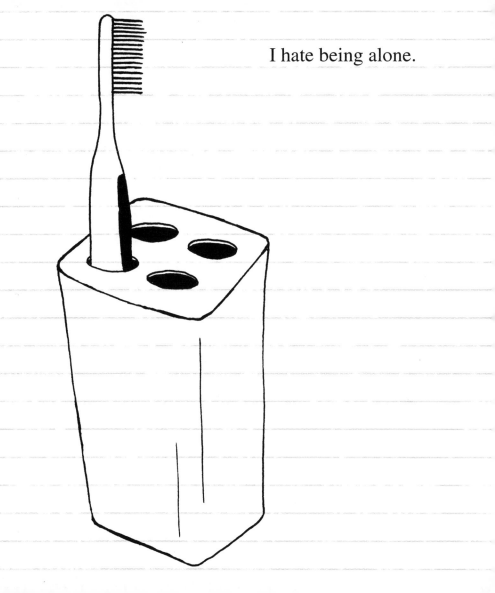

I hate that my neighbors' lawns look awesome.

I hate that I'm not retired so I can't work on my lawn all day too.

I hate that it makes me look like a lazy bum.

I hate when all my surrounding neighbors' homes are for sale.

I hate that my home is smaller than my friends' homes.

I hate that I don't make more money.

I hate that all soap isn't liquid.

I hate using someone else's soap.

I hate when my friends don't clean their toilet bowl rings.

I hate cleaning toilets.

I hate those strands of hair that cling to the shower wall.

I hate that I don't have a maid.

I hate putting up Christmas lights.
I hate when the light strands are all knotted.
I hate that one little bad bulb makes all the
other lights on the strand go out.

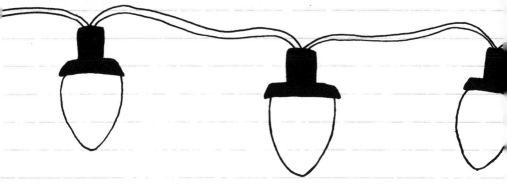

I hate when it's time to take down the
Christmas lights.

I hate when people leave their Christmas lights
up all year long.

I hate that I don't have the audacity to
do that myself.

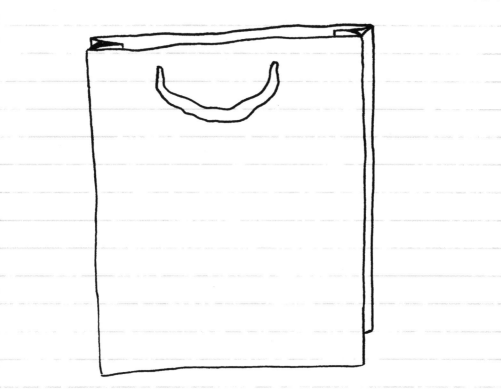

I hate that stores put out back-to-school stuff
while I'm still shopping for a bathing suit.

I hate that I never start my holiday
shopping earlier.

I hate that tissue paper really doesn't
hide the gift.

I hate when reused gift bags have somebody
else's name on them.

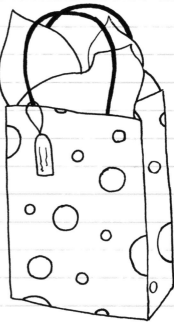

I hate using cool-looking stamps.

I hate that postage keeps going up.

I hate that mailing a letter is still one of the few bargains available.

I hate that it costs the same to mail a letter across the country as it does across the street.

I hate that I don't keep in touch better.

I hate running out of ink.

I hate meaningless Facebook posts.

I hate that you think I care what you're doing right now.

I hate that I don't have more Friends.

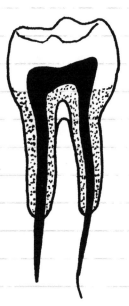

I hate cavities.

I hate getting told every time I go to the dentist that I don't floss enough.

I hate that I don't floss enough.

I hate people who obviously never floss.

I hate taxes.

I hate that politicians can be corrupt.

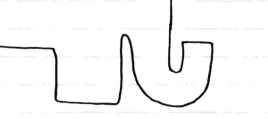

I hate that there's an animal called a jackass.

I hate being politically correct.

I hate trying to open new music CDs.

I hate that every CD case I own is cracked (usually caused by trying to open them).

I hate renting movies that some sticky-fingered kid has drooled on, causing the movie to skip during the best scene.

I hate that skipping is just for kids.

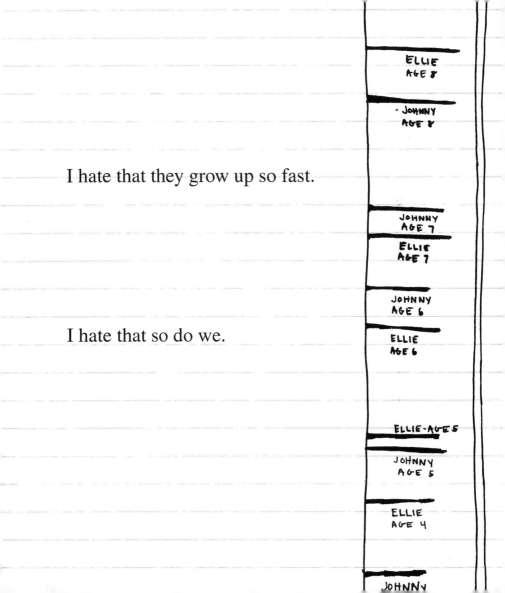

ELLIE
AGE 8

· JOHNNY
AGE 8

I hate that they grow up so fast.

JOHNNY
AGE 7

ELLIE
AGE 7

JOHNNY
AGE 6

I hate that so do we.

ELLIE
AGE 6

ELLIE-AGE 5

JOHNNY
AGE 5

ELLIE
AGE 4

JOHNNY

I hate that shopping carts love being affectionate with my car.

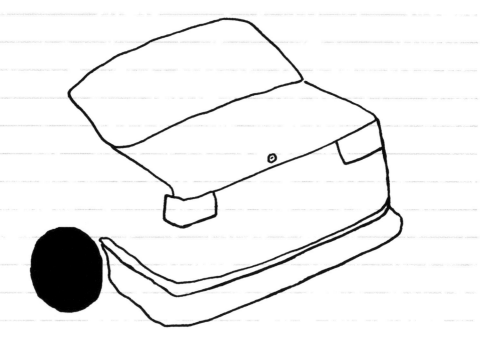

I hate when the heater shuts off and I'm still cold.

I hate changing filters.

I hate allergies.

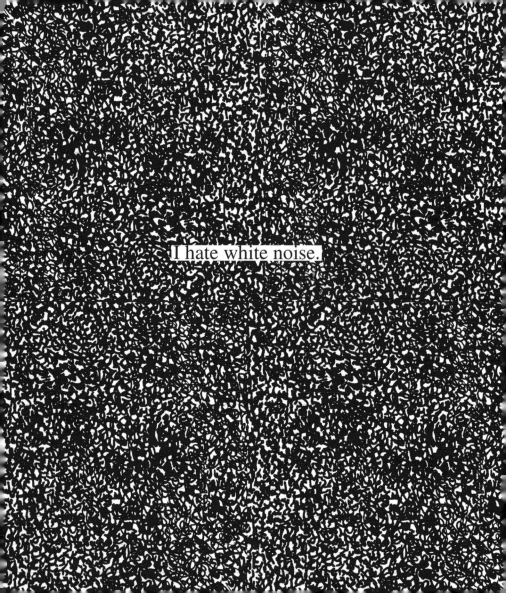
I hate white noise.

I hate silence.

I hate public hot tubs.

I hate the long, unsightly hair that grows
out of moles.

I hate that wool makes me itch.

I hate that I have so many scratch pads.

I hate that I can never find one when I need it.

I hate that everything isn't scratch and sniff.

I hate when you forget a wine bottle opener.

I hate when people enjoy blush as a fine wine.

I hate that people age wine but never drink it.

I hate saving a good bottle for a
special occasion.

I hate that I never have an occasion special
enough for it.

I hate that all wine doesn't age.

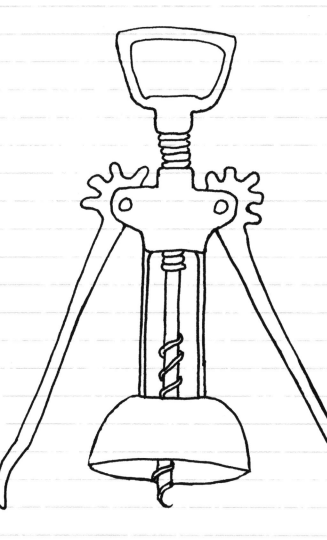

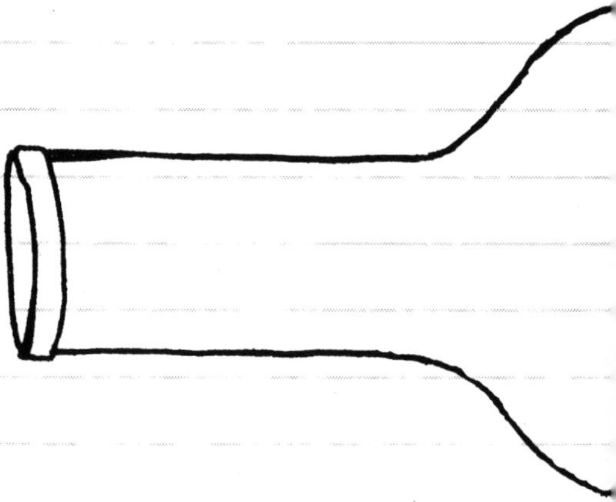

I hate that I never played spin the bottle.

I hate that I have played truth or dare.

I hate it when people are late.

I hate that, no matter how hard I try,
I'm always late.

I hate that I never really could yo-yo.

I hate that other people can make it look so easy and fun.

I hate that the world isn't still flat.

I hate that greedy people have claimed
ownership to the earth's oil.

I hate oil.

I hate that my state bird is so small.

I hate that I never see my
state bird.

I hate that the city smells.

I hate that pizza is so greasy.

I hate that paper plates are so thin.

I hate that my pants aren't oil resistant.

I hate that all fruit isn't seedless.
I hate that all soup isn't chunky.

I hate that all nuts aren't salted.

I hate that they still put beets in salad bars.

I hate when lunchmeat works its way out
of the back of the roll.

I hate when there aren't
turkey leftovers.

I hate that turkeys don't
come bigger.

I hate big family dinners.

I hate that old chocolate gets funky.

I hate that printer ink cartridges cost more than my printer.

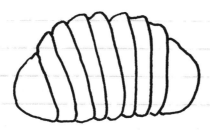

I hate when the waiter can't pronounce *gnocchi*.

I hate that I never get to see a volcano erupt.

I hate that ice cream bends my spoon.

I hate that I still have these same flimsy,
old utensils.

I hate that pots and pans lose their ability
to be nonstick.

I hate that everything isn't nonstick.

I hate seeing people pick their
nose while driving.

I hate that there really isn't a safe place to
pick your nose.

I hate feeling so dirty after riding the subway.

I'd hate the subway if it were clean too.

I hate that I buy the new fashion trends too late.

I hate knowing that there are better options
for everything I own.

I hate that there are dog-breed-specific products with pictures on them that don't look anything like my purebred.

I hate that my dog is always watching me.

I hate that my dog doesn't listen.

I hate that it probably got that from me.

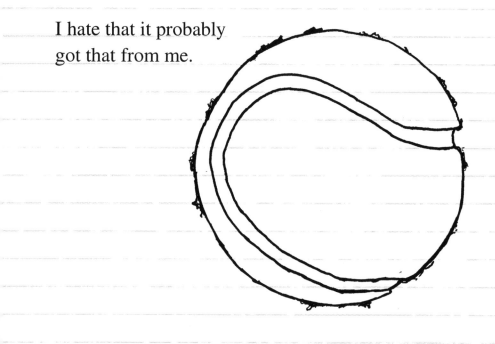

I hate that my dog
can't talk.

I hate that, secretly,
I think cats can talk.

I hate stupid movies that waste two hours
of my life.

I hate that no matter how bad a movie is,
I still need to finish it.

I hate that TiVo wasn't invented
before the VCR.

I hate that my dream was to own a video rental store someday.

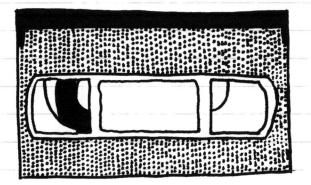

I hate that I did.

I hate that Polaroids are a thing of the past.

I hate that I never developed that roll of film.

I hate that I don't know what's in my
junk drawer.

I hate that I have more than one junk drawer.

I hate that I can't fit a car in my garage.

I hate that there are only fifty-two Saturdays
a year.

I hate that I only get sick on the weekend.

I hate that I don't get snow days off anymore.

I hate that it hasn't snowed since I bought
a snowblower.

I hate that it doesn't snow every Christmas.

I hate morning eye crust.

I hate that I'm always hungry.

I hate that SpaghettiOs are for kids.

I hate that Saturday-morning cartoons aren't nearly as good as they used to be.

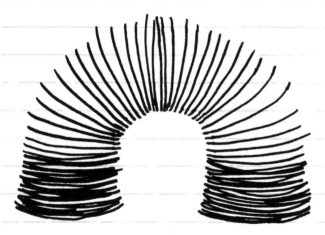

I hate when Slinkies go bad.

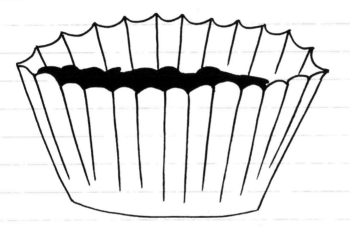

I hate finding grinds in my coffee.
I hate finding stickers on my fruit.
I hate that stickers don't taste better.

I hate licking envelopes.
I hate running out of stamps.
I hate missing the mailman.

I hate junk mail.

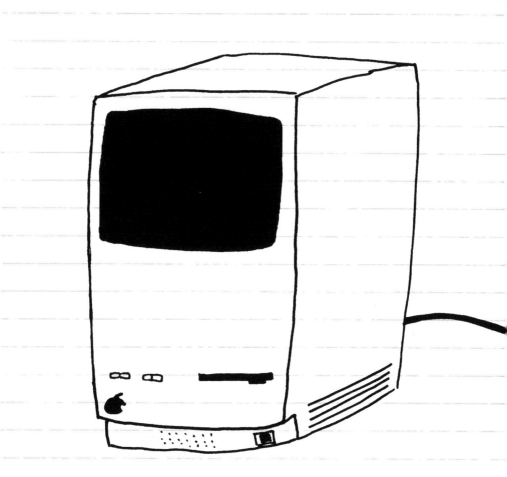

I hate that my computer is already outdated.

I hate that software needs updates.

I hate that I want a flat-screen even though I have a TV with a huge screen.

I hate that I bought everything big, and now smaller is the way to go.

I hate that bigger isn't always better.

I hate slugs.

I hate that "first day of school" smell.

I hate that we still don't get summers off.

I hate when summer is over.

I hate that the city is so close to the suburbs.

I hate that I can hear a highway when
I try to sleep.

I hate that every time
we adjust for daylight-
savings, I seem to lose
an hour of sleep.

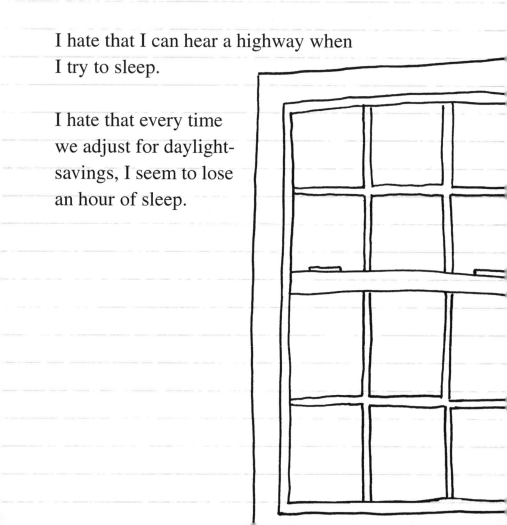

I hate that I have to get up to pee at night.

I hate wetting my bed. (Okay, I don't anymore, but I hate that I used to.)

I hate that I will probably wet my bed again.

I hate that the only good part of an artichoke
is the heart.

I hate that my heart is an open book.
I hate that Frank Sinatra is gone.
I hate that flour is enriched.
I hate that I don't know what it's enriched with.

I hate that alcohol has adverse effects.
I hate that some of those effects are yet
to come.

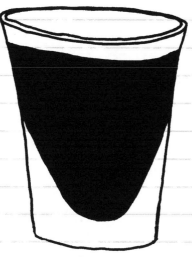

I hate that bar people get more attractive
as the night gets later.
I hate that I don't.

I hate stupid souvenirs.
I hate when people don't bring me back
a souvenir.

I hate cruise ship photos.
I hate that I look so good in every picture that
I have to buy them all.

I hate that I can never refold a map.

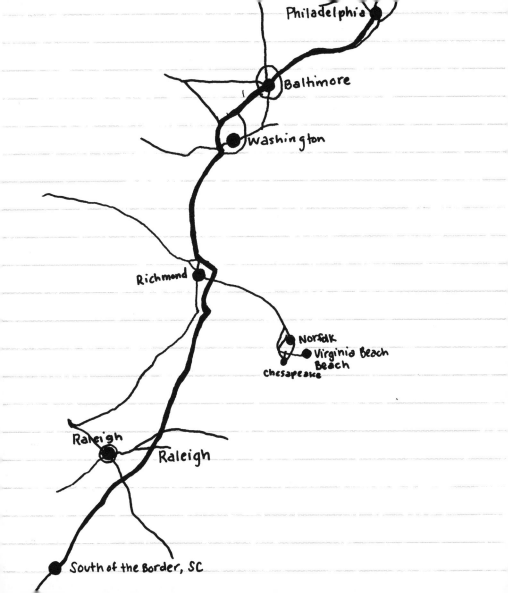

I hate looking into an empty fridge—again—
and hoping something will appear.

I hate that mini-fridges aren't bigger.

I hate finding an empty ice-cube tray.

I hate that Vanilla Ice still doesn't kick out more catchy tunes like "Ice-Ice Baby."

I hate that they took the awards away
from Milli Vanilli.

I hate that I can't blame it on the rain.

I hate stretching.
I hate combination locks.
I hate that locker-room smell.
I hate pretending that I like sports.

I hated showering after gym class.
I hated that I developed late.
I hated that they developed early.
I hated puberty.

I hate that one is bigger than the other.

I hate that you know what I mean.

I hate when people ask you for help because
you are good at something.

I hate helping people move.

I hate when they don't help you on your
moving day.

I hate that I carpeted my home with
trendy colors.

I hate that I didn't know magenta and turquoise
were going to be trendy.

- I hate that pasta sauce is attracted to white.
- I hate that whiteout takes so long to dry.
- I hate that I can't reach the number keys when typing.
- I hate that if it's not on a list, I forget.
- I hate lists.

I hate not knowing everything.

I hate that people still call me a smart-ass.

I hate that people don't realize I'm always right.

I hate that cheating on exams wasn't easier.

I hate playing by the rules.

I hate that I never learned to drive a stick shift.
I hate seeing big, seven-passenger SUVs with
one person in them.
I hate that "blood rushing to your head" feeling
when police car lights come on behind you.
I hate when the cop rushes past you after you
get that feeling—for no reason.

I hate that my fireplace doesn't burn wood.

I hate public displays of affection.

I hate that people aren't more romantic.

I hate that you have to take three aspirin . . .
why not just make one big one?

I hate swallowing horse-sized pills.

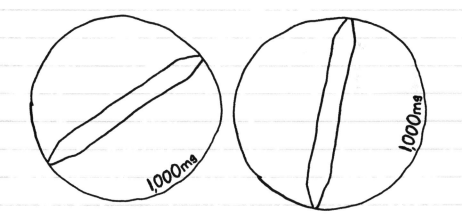

I hate the smell of a smoker's car.

I hate that the word *ginormous* officially
became a word.
I hate school loans.
I hate that school loans are so . . . *dammit* . . .
ginormous.

I hate parents who don't talk about anything
else but their kids.
I hate that I don't have kids to have anything
to talk about with them.
I hate that you now know that I don't have kids.
I hate that you've already assumed that
I don't have kids.
I hate you for making me think about
the snot-nosed brats I still don't have.

I hate kids.

I hate bags of chips that only have four and a half chips in them.

I hate that my home-cooked fries don't taste like McDonald's.

I hate that nobody really knows if salt is good or bad for you.

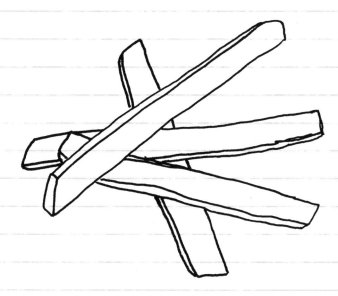

I hate that I love salt.

I hate finding lipstick on my diner coffee mug.

I hate leaving a tip for someone who doesn't deserve it.

I hate when I don't get a tip.

I hate when people give you unwanted advice.

I hate when someone gets to the free stuff before I do.

I hate that my cassette player takes up
valuable space.

I hate that I keep it around for the one cassette
I might play someday.

I hate that I don't know where my cassettes are.

I hate that my teen mix tape was probably left in a car I sold years ago.

I hate that someone else is still laughing at the songs I had on that tape.

I hate being the chauffeur because I have the largest car.

I hate that nobody kicks in for gas money.

I hate that the Internet wasn't around when I was in school.

I hate that technology keeps getting smaller, but my fingers stay the same size.

I hate that babies have fat fingers.

I hate that wind chimes don't always chime.
I hate the wind.
I hate that you saw that coming.
I hate being predictable.

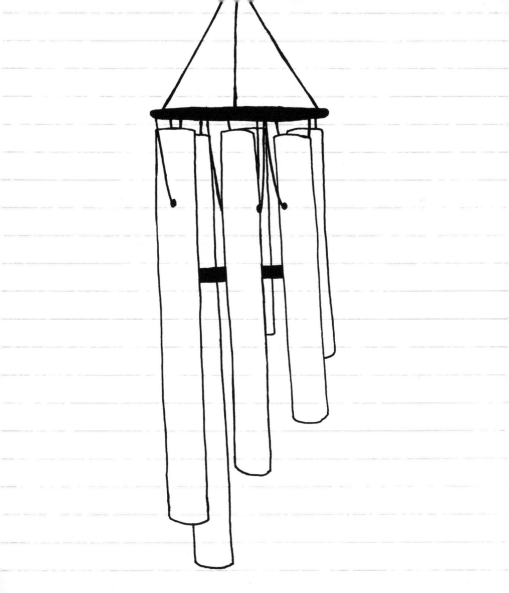

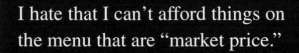

I hate that I can't afford things on the menu that are "market price."

I hate that seafood tastes like the sea.

I hate that sunsets are prettiest on
tropical islands.

I hate that I don't have more vacation time.

I hate that after watching *Titanic*
four times they didn't see the
iceberg any sooner, not even once.

I hate that Rose didn't make
room for Jack on that piece of wood.

I hate that she said she wouldn't let go,
but did.

I hate that you know I liked *Titanic*.*

*It was for the historic aspect, I assure you.

hat there is a first class.
hat coach doesn't have any class.
hat neither do I.

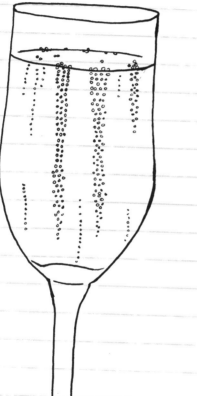

I hate that you know I'd be lying if I told you I
didn't cry each time I watched *Titanic*.

I hate that I can't blame that on dust in the air.

I hate dust.

I hate t
I hate t
I hate t

I hate that the air on a plane has to be recycled.

I hate that the cool stuff to see is always on the other side of the plane.

I hate that there aren't enough pillows.

I hate the fear that the airline lost my luggage—again.

I hate that my carry-on never fits.

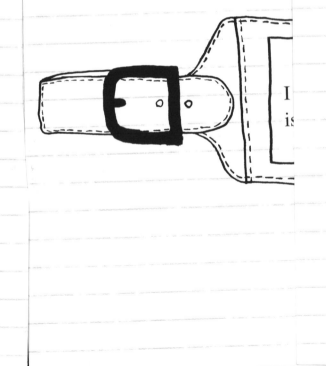

I hate that I hated school.

I hate that I want to go back to college.

I hate that teachers don't get paid more.

I hate that I don't get paid more.

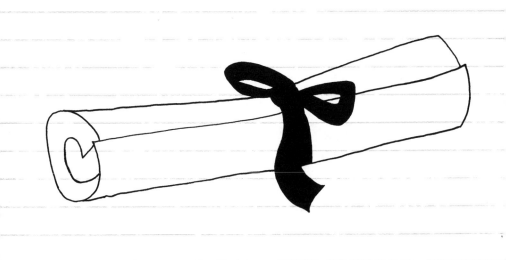

I hate that I never discovered dinosaur bones.

I hate that scary movies
keep me up at night.

I hate that when I pull
the covers over my head,
I feel safe.

I hate knowing that is so
not true.

I hate when I run out of dryer sheets.

I hate that all shirts aren't wrinkle-free.

I hate starched clothes.

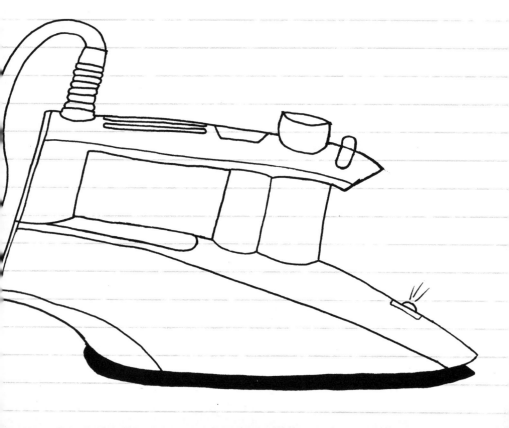

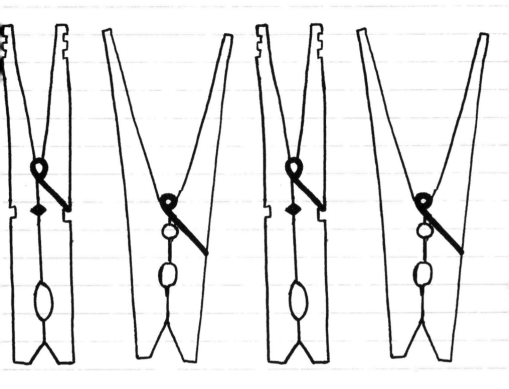

I hate clotheslines.
I hate that you can't see them in the dark.
I hate outdoor motion lights.

I hate that my dog doesn't bark
when someone is at the door.

I hate that other dogs bark when
I walk by their houses.

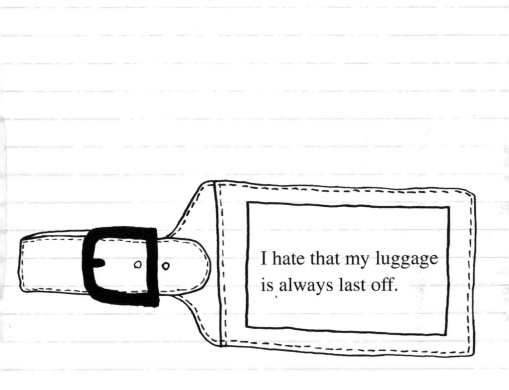

I hate that there is a first class.
I hate that coach doesn't have any class.
I hate that neither do I.

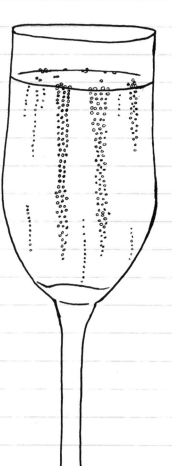

I hate that you know I'd be lying if I told you I didn't cry each time I watched *Titanic*.

I hate that I can't blame that on dust in the air.

I hate dust.

I hate that the air on a plane has to be recycled.

I hate that the cool stuff to see is always on the other side of the plane.

I hate that there aren't enough pillows.

I hate the fear that the airline lost my luggage—again.

I hate that my carry-on never fits.

I hate that I can't nap more often.
I hate feeling guilty about having a lazy day.
I hate that I can't sleep in because there is
something that I should be doing.

I hate being accused that I don't help around the house.

I hate doing things around the house.

I hate that TV is so irresistible.

I hate when someone invents something that I thought of first.

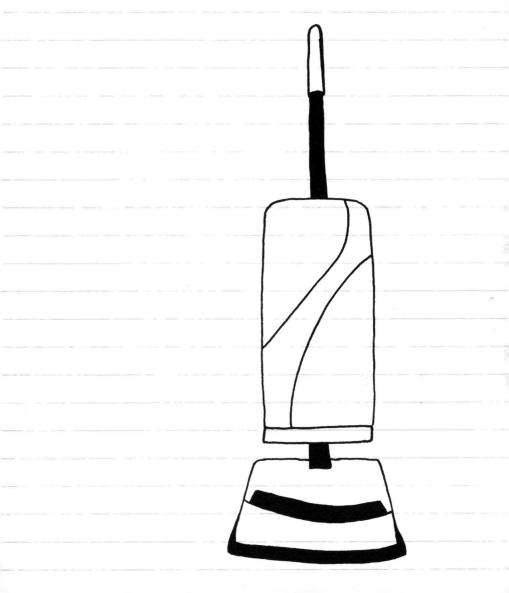

I hate throwing parties.
I hate that my parties have gotten a lot smaller.
I hate when people don't RSVP.
I hate when people bring uninvited guests.
I hate when there isn't enough food at a party.
I hate when people take home what they
brought to a party.

I hate party poopers.

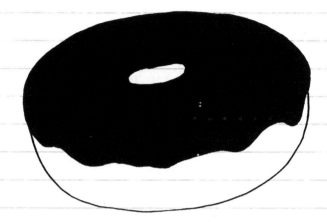

I hate that more chocolate-glazed donuts don't
come in the assortment box.

I hate fantasy sports leagues.
I hate that all light switches aren't dimmers.
I hate when good TV shows go off the air.
I hate that they ruin good TV shows with
nonstop syndication.

I hate people who make computer viruses.

I hate that these people don't do something
good with their talents.

I hate that I don't have that talent.

I hate overanalyzing things.

I hate concert seating.

I hate that cell phone screens have replaced lighters at concerts.

I hate bootleg, poor-quality, concert T-shirts sold in the parking lot.

I hate that those shirts are too good of a deal to pass up.

I hate that I feel compelled to buy those overpriced event books.

I hate that I never look at those books again.

I hate that everyone doesn't tailgate.

I hate concert parking.

I hate when my ears ring after a concert.

I hate feeling old.

I hate that you can't sell everything on eBay.

I hate hoping I get a good eBay rating.

I hate that I can't seem to make any money on eBay, but I still try.

I hate paying for intangible services.

I hate all the hours I personally wasted vacuuming.

I hate that the Roomba would get my allowance now.

I hate that when I used to cut the lawn I'd get a lousy couple of bucks.

I hate that kids now expect $25.

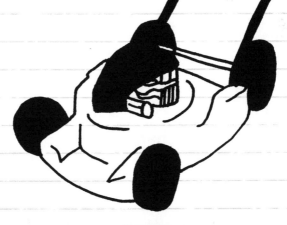

I hate inflation.

I hate infatuation.

I hate that nobody is infatuated with me.

I hate that I'm infatuated with movie stars.

I hate that I'm not
a movie star.

I hate that I can't sing.

I hate that I like to sing.

I hate people who think they can sing.

I hate that I don't have a fancy stage name.

I hate that I never owned a zoot suit.
I hate that I really don't know what a
zoot suit is.
I hate that I'll never be in a zoot suit riot.

I hate that I missed the chance to party like
it was 1999.

I hate that they never found the beef.
I hate overplayed commercials.
I hate jingles that you can't get out of
your head.

I hate that everybody doesn't know that the
bird, bird, bird; the bird is the word.

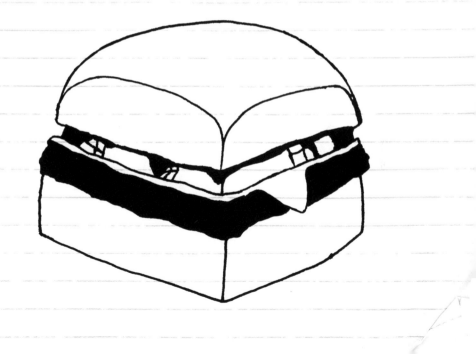

I hate that I can be so annoying.

I hate it when people get on my last nerve.

I hate that Willy Wonka still freaks me out.

I hate all the therapy that Oompa Loompas
caused kids around the world.

I hate that I don't have a corner window office
in the big city overlooking the park.
I hate that all jobs aren't like in the movies.
I hate that I watch way too many movies.
I hate that I'll never chase a tornado.
I hate that there is no place like home.

I hate that I've never followed a yellow
brick road.
I hate that the White House doesn't have more
of a clever name.
I hate color-coded systems.

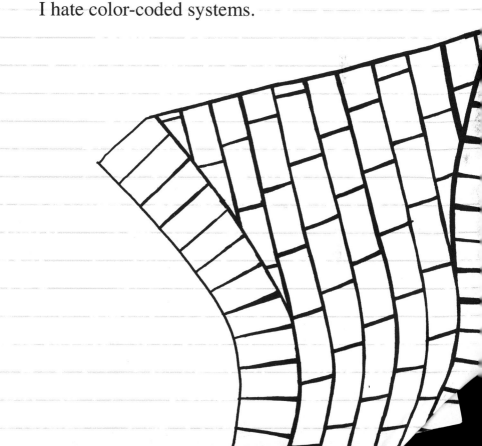

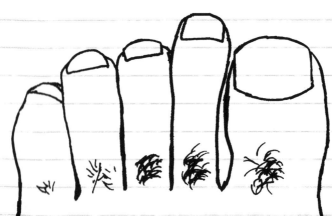

I hate when the longest toe isn't the big toe.

I hate that I never read the magazines
I subscribe to.

I hate that all books don't have pictures.

I hate when my cell phone battery runs out in
the middle of

I hate that I don't have more time to play
video games.
I hate that I never beat a video game.
I hate that video game consoles only come with
one controller.
I hate accessories.
I hate that I can't accessorize.

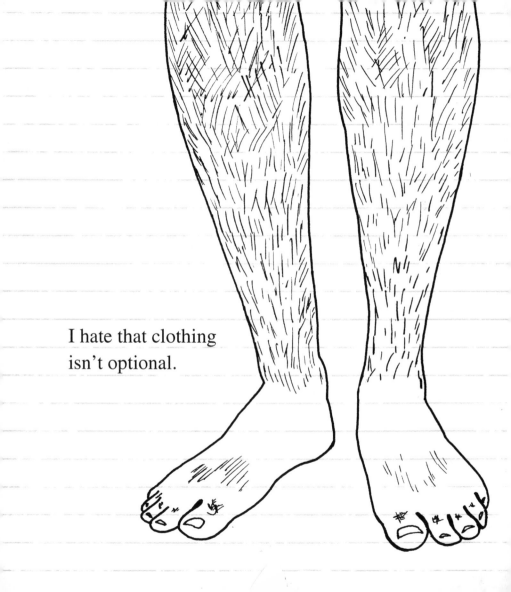

I hate that clothing
isn't optional.

I hate tolls.

I hate that elves don't really bake cookies.
I hate that all cookies aren't soft and chewy.

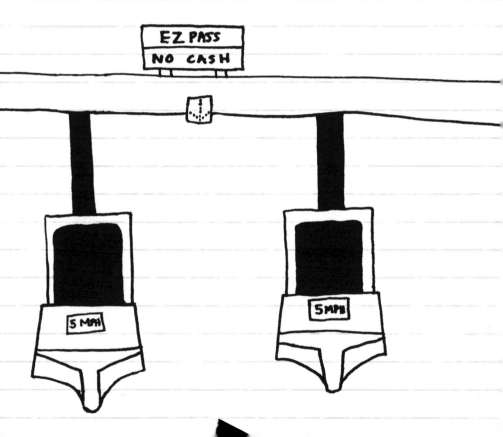

I hate that I don't have
magic beans.
I hate that there is no magic
genie inside my lamp.
I hate that three wishes
wouldn't be enough.
I hate that Humpty Dumpty
was foolish enough to sit
on a wall.
I hate that nursery rhymes
can be horrific.

I hate that I'm not in someone's will.

I hate having to go first.

I hate coming in last.

I hate that I'll never be in
the Olympics.

I hate that I thought I would.

I hate that all takeout food doesn't come in Chinese food containers.

I hate that every meal doesn't come with a fortune cookie.

I hate that my lucky number doesn't work for me.

I hate that I never found a four-leaf clover.

I hate bad wedding speeches.
I hate that I don't have my own identity.
I hate that all diamonds aren't identical.
I hate that I have flaws.

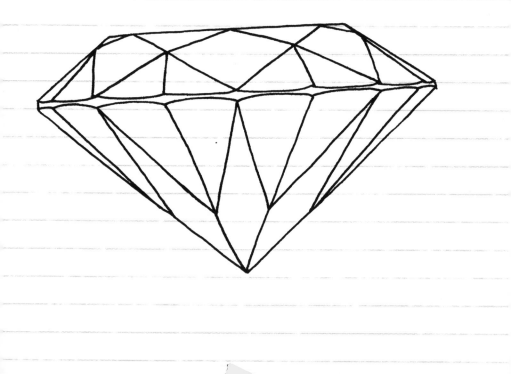

I hate that I didn't find the One Ring that will rule them all.

I hate that I'll never be the Lord of the Ring.

I hate that I don't know how many lords are a-leaping.

I hate people who can't keep secrets.
I hate gossip.
I hate being the last to know.
I hate quitters.
I hate that I don't try harder.

I hate that what doesn't kill me hasn't made me stronger.

I hate seeing lovebirds canoodle.
I hate that nobody canoodles with me.
I hate when noodles stick together.
I hate being a stick in the mud.
I hate that my life is so boring.
I hate getting too excited.

I hate that you can spell *catsup* in more than
one way.
I hate when people put ketchup on everything.

WHAT DO YOU CALL A PIECE OF
WOOD WITH NOTHING TO DO?

BOARD.

I hate that more food doesn't come on a stick.
I hate when my ice cream cone leaks.
I hate that I can't put rainbow sprinkles
on everything.

I hate that rainbows only come
out when it rains.
I hate that I'm only happy
when it rains.
I hate when songs get stuck in
your head.
I hate when MY iPod plays
a song I really don't like.
I hate that I don't have a good
P'P'P'Poker Face.

I hate that my car doesn't transform into
a big robot.

I hate that the bank drive-through teller
stopped giving me lollipops.

I hate that I'll never be in a boy band.

I hate that I don't get sent
to my room anymore.
I hate that yawns are contagious.
Yawn. . . .

I hate that I don't remember
all of my dreams.
I hate that all of my dreams
haven't come true.

I hate that I have recurring dreams about going to school in my underwear.

I hate tighty-whities.

I hate running out of staples.

I hate having to use those awful
left-handed scissors.

I hate that I can't write left-handed.

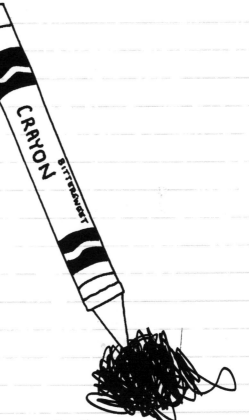

I hate coloring between the lines.

I hate that my mind thinks faster than
I can type.

I hate that adult diapers aren't cool to try.

I hate that it took so long for thongs to catch on.

I hate that my theme song doesn't play when
I walk around.

I hate when squirrels eat all the bird food.
I hate that mosquitoes use the birdbath more
than the birds.
I hate, hate, *hate* mosquitoes.
I hate that mosquitoes love, love, *love* me.

I hate missing trash day.

I hate running the trash out at the last minute
in my bathrobe.

I hate that beauty magazines make me feel fat.

I hate that I never had a pony.

I hate losing buttons.

I hate that I never replace
lost buttons.

I hate that baseball caps look silly on me.
I hate the word *cap*.

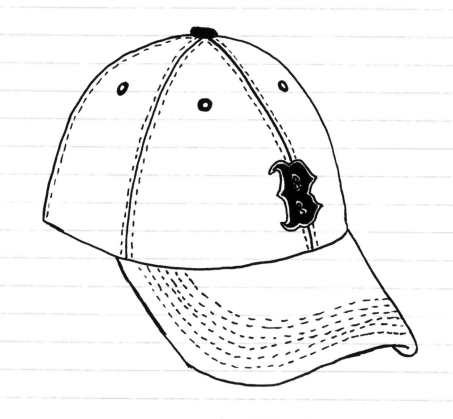

I hate that eyes don't have a zoom feature.

I hate that I can't put in contact lenses.

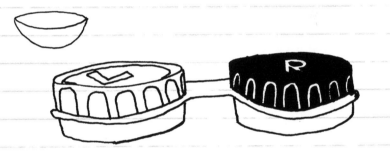

I hate that laser eye surgery isn't guaranteed.

I hate that life doesn't have an undo button.

I hate cold feet.

I hate movies based on true stories.
I hate that my life isn't interesting enough
to have a movie based on it.
I hate that too many child stars have tough
lives when they grow up.
I hate parents who put their kids into
show business.

I hate that my parents didn't put
me into show business.

I hate when spoiled rich people
complain about their woes.

I hate that I don't have rich woes
to complain about.

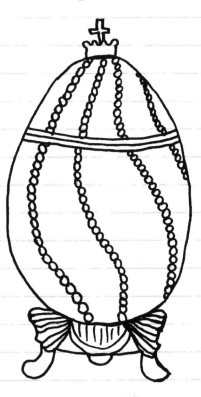

I hate that there isn't always pie ready
for dessert.
I hate that potpies sound better than they taste.
I hate burning the roof of my mouth.
I hate that movie theater popcorn smells
so good.
I hate that it's not real butter.
I hate stepping on scales.

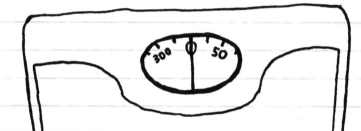

I hate that all jeans don't make me look good.

I hate when clothing-store
dummy bodies are sexier than mine.

I hate climbing wobbly, old
wooden ladders.

I hate that everything has a dot-com.
I hate that all the good dot-coms
are taken.

I hate that dandelions are so pretty, then days
later so atrocious.
I hate that no matter how many you pluck,
more keep coming back.
I hate that my neighbors don't care how many
dandelions they have.

I hate that one person can make a difference.
I hate that I'm not that person.
I hate that I don't know that person.

I hate people who have too many items in the
10-Items-or-Less line.

I hate self-checkout lines.

I hate that they still need people to work the
self-checkout lines.

I hate that all movies aren't as good as *Braveheart*.

I hate that people no longer carry around swords.

I hate that we don't hear bagpipes more often.

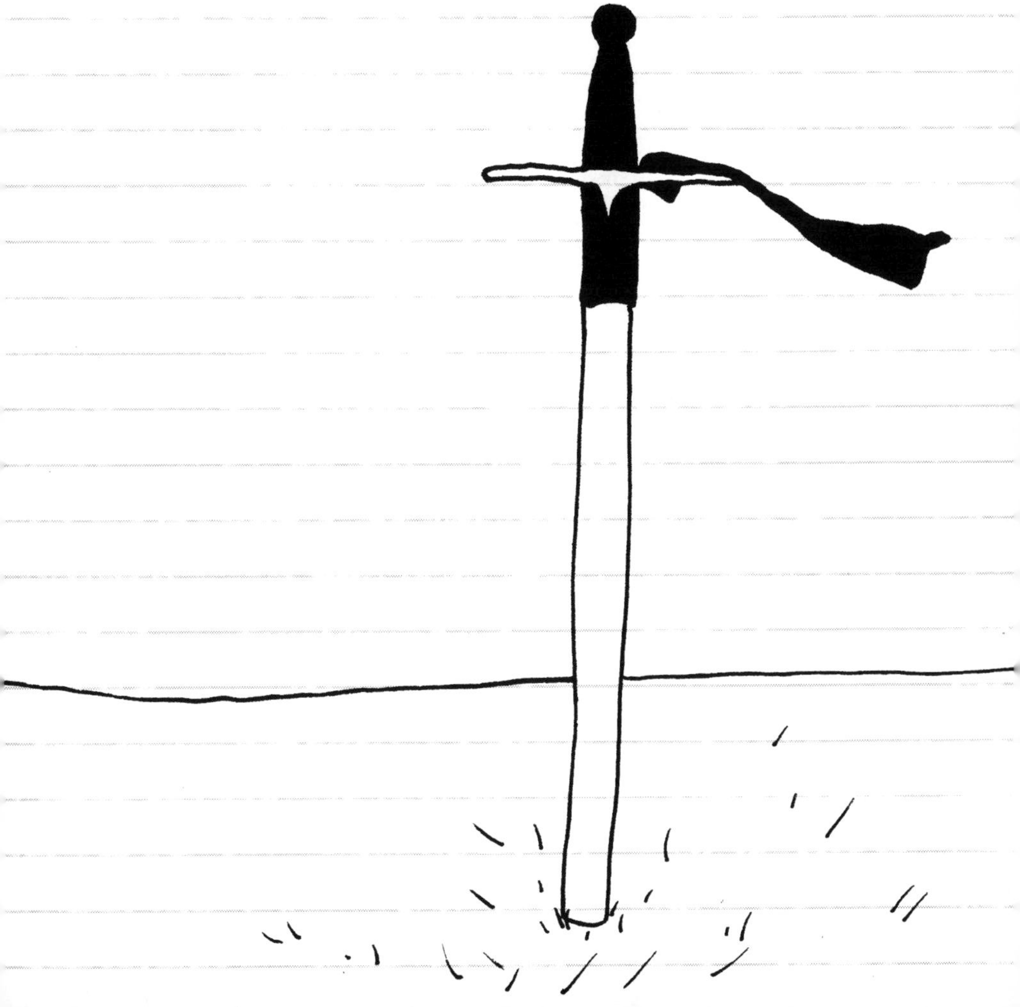

I hate musical prodigies.

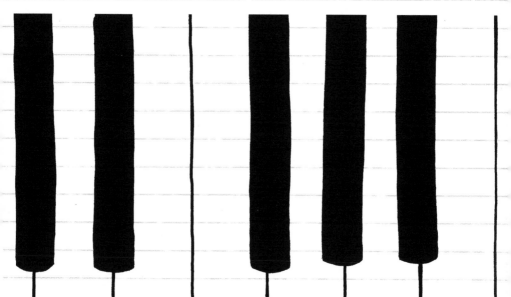

I hate that more women don't wear flowers in
their hair.
I hate that every place isn't like Disney World.
I hate that all mint ice cream isn't green.
I hate feeling obligated to help old people
shovel snow.

I hate scraping ice from car windows.

I hate the saying "don't let the bedbugs bite."
I hate knowing bedbugs exist.

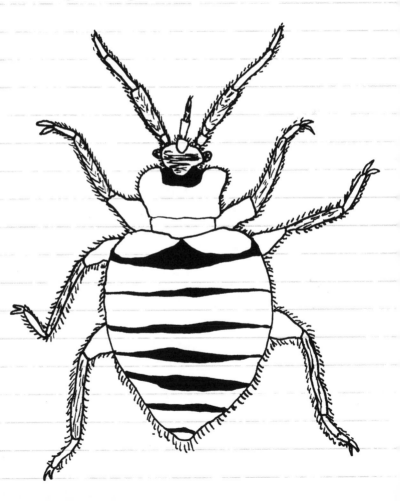

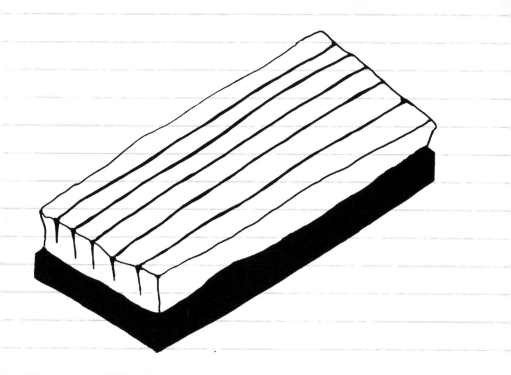

I hate when people don't cover their mouths
when sneezing.
I hate when people don't say, "Bless you."
I hate clapping chalkboard erasers.

I hate Japanese beetles.

I hate New Year's resolutions.

I hate installing fences.

I hate that AM radio isn't more popular.

I hate that it rains the day after I wash my car.

I hate the classifieds.

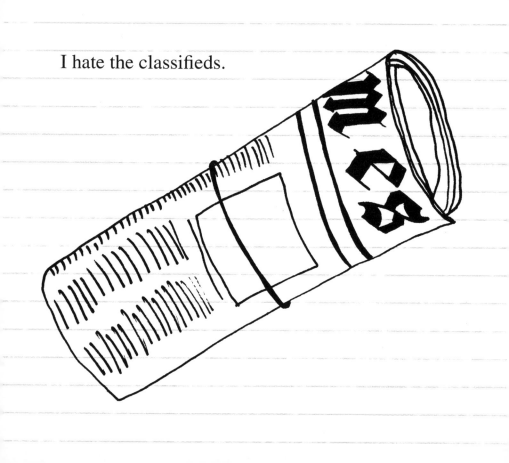

I hate that all snow isn't made
for snowballs.

I hate that snowmen melt.

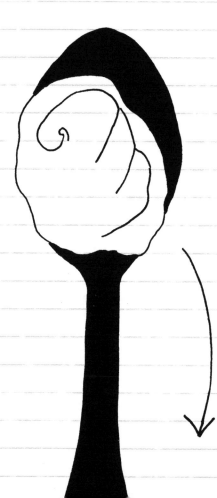

I hate that I've never been in a food fight.

I hate that I've had to clean up after
a food fight.

I hate bad Christmas cookies.
I hate hollow chocolate Easter bunnies.
I hate when I run out of trick-or-treat candy . . .
before Halloween.

I hate that green beer comes only once a year.
I hate that there aren't other colors of beer.

I hate toaster oven crumbs.

I hate cluttered refrigerator doors.

I hate forgetting about leftovers in the fridge.

I hate how plastic containers get when you microwave them.

I hate that you can't microwave metal.

I hate that I found that out the hard way.

I hate my alarm clock.

I hate creepy basements.

I hate drop ceilings.

I hate wood paneling.

I hate living rooms that you aren't allowed
to enter.

I hate that more potatoes don't fit in a
five-pound bag.

I hate how the mind can wander.

I hate customer service.

I hate automated phone systems.

I hate hang-up calls.

I hate cell phone contracts.

I hate when people drive while talking on the phone.

I hate seeing people stranded on the side of a road.

I hate that I don't stop to help them.

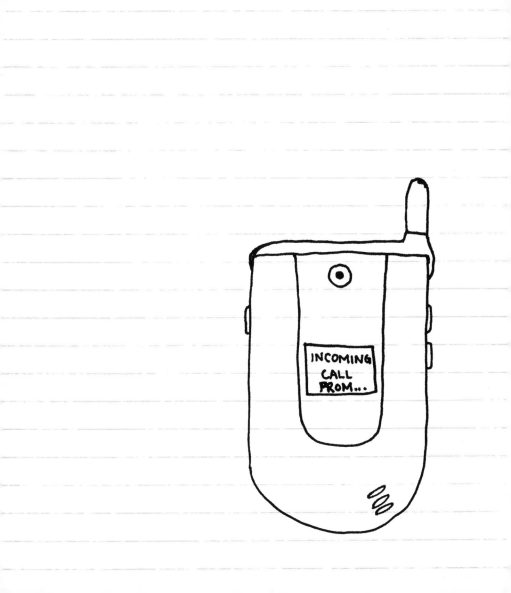

I hate that I never cruised around in a jeep
without doors.
I hate waiting in lines at the gas station.
I hate that it takes so long to pump gas.
I hate when lanes merge.
I hate daytime roadwork.
I hate rush hour.
I hate rushing.

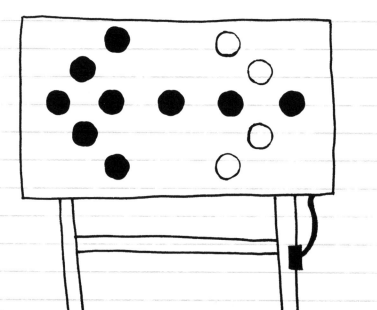

I hate nose hair.

I hate topiaries.

I hate weeds.

I hate that weeds grow faster than the lawn.

I hate that weeds are considered ugly.

I hate digging holes.

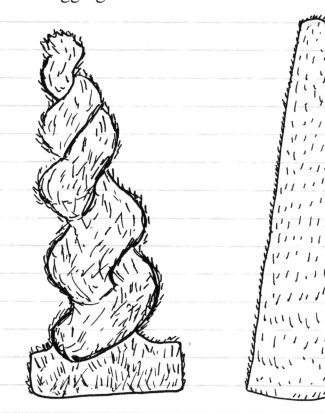

I hate dirt under fingernails.
I hate dry lips.
I hate bad kissers.
I hate that nobody has ever told me that
I kiss good.
I hate bad breath.
I hate not knowing I have bad breath.

I hate that all pickles aren't crunchy.

I hate that everything doesn't come with
a pickle.

I hate when you bite into a dill pickle and find
out it's sweet.

I hate that they pickle things other than pickles.

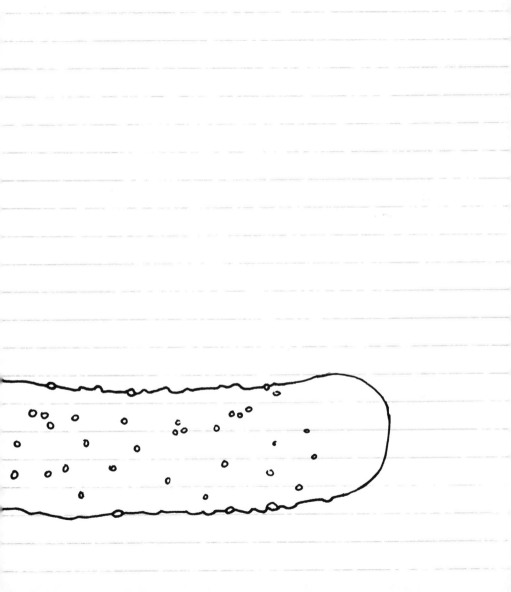

I hate getting Canadian coins with my change.
I hate when the ATM is out of money.
I hate ATM fees.
I hate owing money.
I hate wasting gym memberships.
I hate that working out really isn't working out.

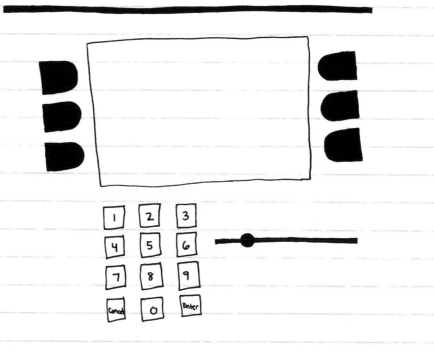

I hate when gift cards expire.
I hate getting gift cards as gifts.
I hate when there is no thought behind a gift.
I hate when people re-gift.
I hate when things go unappreciated.
I hate complainers.

I hate not being cool or hot.
I hate that surfing is so cool,
yet so hard.

I hate that smell from under a cast.
I hate that my body doesn't heal
as quickly anymore.
I hate that you don't realize this
when you're young.

I hate getting things started.

I hate that I've never really finished anythi

I hate having nine hundred TV channels and
still nothing to watch.
I hate that I scroll through the channels twice
to make sure.
I hate when my remote loses its battery cover.
I hate having to turn on the TV manually.
I hate when I find the missing battery cover,
but can't find my remote.

I hate using tape to fix things.

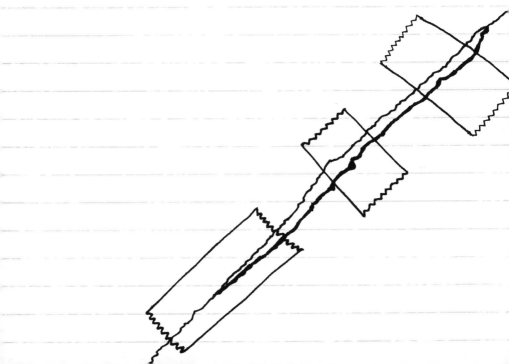

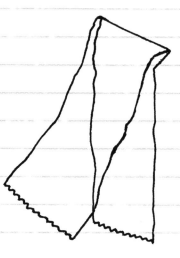

I hate when the tape runs out and I need one more piece.
I hate when tape sticks together.

I hate that I have to steal another roll of tape from the office.

I hate loaning things out.

I hate asking for things back that I've
loaned out.

I hate that *Monopoly* money
doesn't look more real.

I hate not being able to pass
"Go" or collect $200.

I hate that all my board games
smell like the basement.

I hate that I don't know how to play
an instrument.
I hate taking the long way home.
I hate that I fear the reaper.

I hate that there aren't more
commandments.
I hate that thunder automatically
generates fear.
I hate that there aren't more music
videos like "Thriller."

I hate that some people get a star on the Hollywood Walk of Fame who clearly don't deserve one.

I hate that they don't just give
Oscars to the old actors.
(This might be their last chance!)

Have I mentioned I hate
getting old?

I hate that they cut speeches
short at the awards shows.

I hate that awards shows go
on too long.

I hate when they pair movie stars together
for comedies.
I hate that they don't put them back together
again in more movies.
I hate romantic comedies.
I hate that it still isn't the Renaissance period.
I hate sequels.

I hate that lightsabers don't
really exist.

I hate that fairy tales don't
come true.

I hate when people watch a dog do its business.

I hate that people see my dog do its business
in their yard.

I hate when dogs do their business in my yard.

I hate when the sheets aren't fresh.
I hate changing the bed.
I hate the pressure of Valentine's Day.

I hate that Easter isn't as big as Christmas.
I hate that people don't make a big deal out of
my birthday.

I hate empty cookie jars.

I hate that other careers pay more than mine.
I hate that my guidance counselor didn't
tell me that.

I hate that it's harder and
harder to get into the holiday spirit.
I hate when I miss my favorite holiday
TV shows.
I hate that they don't play *A Christmas Story*
all year long.

I hate when old men whistle.

I hate seeing old people hold hands.

I hate when your date points that out.

I hate double-dating.

I hate being more interested in the other person's date.

I hate being compared to exes.

I hate that my Spidey senses don't tingle.

I hate kissing people upside down.

I hate that the hero always gets the girl.

I hate that capes aren't in fashion.

I hate that I'm never the hero.

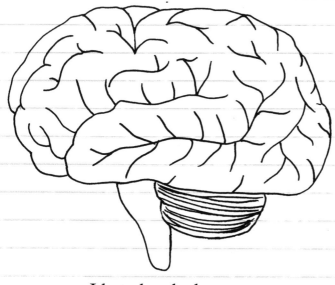

I hate headaches.

I hate when people use a headache as
an excuse.

I hate that most online searches reveal porn.
I hate that you can't be online everywhere.
I hate that Big Brother is watching.

I hate that I don't still own my first car.

I hate shopping carts with a bum wheel.
I hate price checks.
I hate when things at the dollar store cost more
than a dollar.
I hate when people ask: "How much did that
set you back?"

I hate finding out that someone won the lottery, before I checked my ticket.

I hate thinking that I'll actually hit the lottery.

I hate jury duty.
I hate sneezing fits.
I hate when people cough in church.

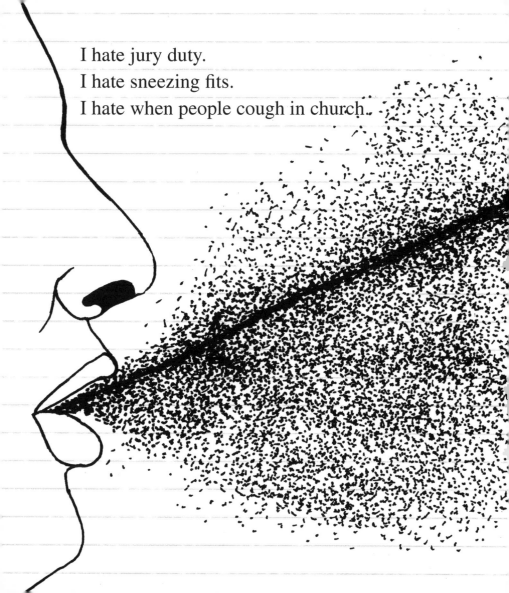

I hate trendy kid names.

I hate when babies cry.

I hate that all children
don't have leashes.

I hate that psychiatrists' lives
are just as messed up as ours.

I hate losing the car keys.
I hate losing games.
I hate sore losers.

I hate being the center of attention.
I hate when I'm not the life of the party
. . . but I hate when my date is.

I hate boxed sets.

I hate collector's editions.

I hate that everything I've ever collected
is incomplete.

I hate that everything I've ever collected
is in storage.

I hate to part with my collections.

I hate that the things I've decided to collect
never went up in value.

I hate return policies.
I hate knowing other people may have tried
on these clothes too.
I hate hand-me-downs.
I hate that thrift stores have nicer clothes
than mine.

I hate banging my funny bone.
I hate that it's not funny at all.
I hate grinning and bearing it.
I hate that I don't live off the wild.
I hate bugs.

I hate that I can't turn people off like a robot.

I hate that I turn people off.

I hate that butter isn't always soft.
I hate that stick butter doesn't need to
be refrigerated.
I hate cleaning the grill.
I hate pulling hair out of a drain.
I hate flushing dead fish.

I hate emptying the dishwasher.
I hate that I have a dishwasher, but still put
dirty dishes in the sink.
I hate when I've been told I filled the
dishwasher wrong.

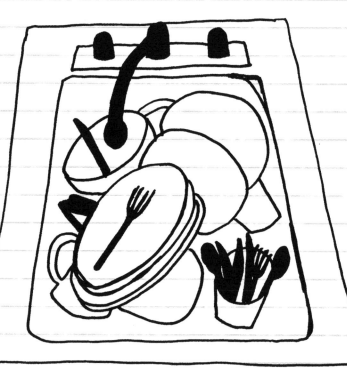

I hate that Dylan left *90210*.
I hate that I knew when to clap during the intro
theme song.
I hate that nobody knows my zip code.
I hate that TV shows are never set in
my hometown.

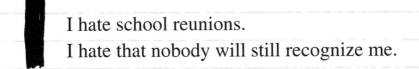

I hate school reunions.
I hate that nobody will still recognize me.

I hate talking to smart people.

I hate that I say dumb things when trying to sound smart.

I hate uncomfortable silence.

I hate that the volume doesn't go any louder.

I hate that I never get to yell *Bingo!*

I hate getting nervous to ask someone out
on a date.
I hate rejection.
I hate that I don't get to reject others.

I hate having a conscience.

I hate that you don't believe that I even have
a conscience.

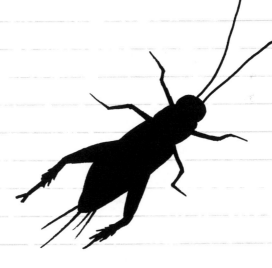

I hate serious comic strips.
I hate that I can't draw people.

I hate that grunge took the fun out
of '80s glam music.
I hate that MTV doesn't play videos.
I hate that someone else ultimately has control.

I hate contracts.
I hate negotiations.
I hate that someone else profits from
negotiations.
I hate that I'm not a good negotiator.
I hate that when I try to haggle, it usually costs
me more.

I hate cauliflower.
I hate food that doesn't have any taste.
I hate that you can't leave the table until you
clean your plate.
I hate that my stomach knows that
it's lunchtime.

I hate misunderstandings.
I hate losing arguments.
I hate that Dad is always right.

I hate that brief moment just after a paper cut
when you know the agony is about to set in.
I hate that splinters nearly cripple me.
I hate when people get shot on TV and it looks
like my splinters hurt more.

I hate inflatable yard decorations.
I hate that I'm not a marksman.

I hate losing my cell phone signal.

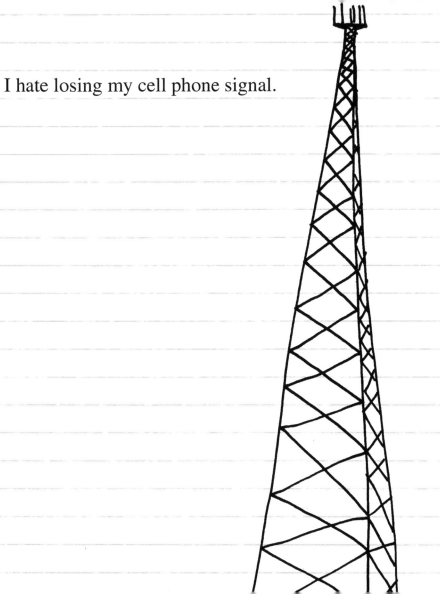

I hate that everything isn't wireless.
I hate losing money in vending machines.
I hate that bottled water costs as much
as soft drinks.
I hate not really knowing where
bottled water comes from.

I hate missing birthdays.

I hate that e-mail has replaced mailing cards.

I hate that cards cost so much.

I hate that I lose so many pens.

I hate that I have to use cheap pens.

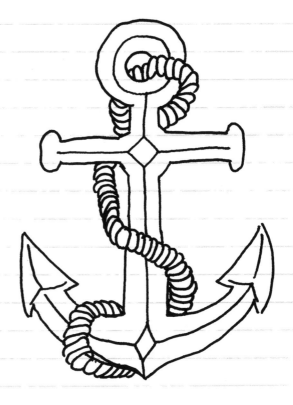

I hate that old tattoos turn blue.
I hate that I'm not brave.
I hate the jazz music that doesn't jive together.

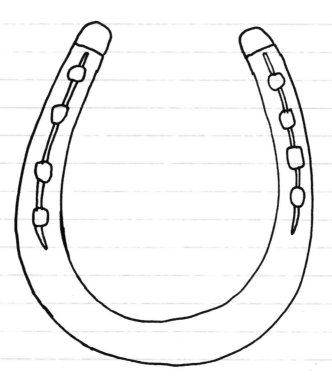

I hate sweepstakes.
I hate that I never win—anything.
I hate that some people are luckier than others.

I hate that we all just don't get along.

I hate sarcasm.

I hate when I don't know that you're being sarcastic.

I hate that it's not polite to touch people.
I hate people that get all touchy-feely when
they drink.
I hate that you can't be tipsy all of the time.
I hate that some people seem like they are.
I hate the smell of booze on someone's breath.
I hate that I'm jealous of them.

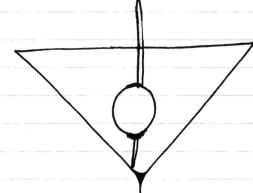

I hate humidity.

I hate sticking to the car seat.

I hate fake leather.

I hate round ottomans.

I hate the word *ottoman*.

I hate when furniture doesn't fit.

I hate that my friends don't just stop by anymore.

I hate when people
stop by unannounced.

I hate credit scores.
I hate credit limits.
I hate that people can steal your identity.
I hate that I don't know how to steal an identity.
I hate my own identity.
I hate that my identity isn't good enough
to steal.

I hate jealousy.

I hate that love is often
the inspiration and demise
of great people.

I hate love songs.

I hate that nobody
wrote a song about me.

I hate that I'm so vain.

I hate insurance.
I hate that your insurance goes up
when you finally use it.

I hate that I didn't read the fine print.

I hate not being royalty.

I hate that I didn't appreciate
the Beatles sooner.
I hate that I don't own a pair of Elvis glasses.
I hate leaving Las Vegas.

I hate that the grass is always greener.
I hate learning the hard way.
I hate that payback's always a bitch.
I hate that nothing good is easy.
I hate looking on the bright side.

I hate picking myself up and dusting
myself off.
I hate getting back up on that horse.
I hate snapping out of it.
I hate that there are more fish in the sea.
I hate clichés.

I hate that there are so many things to hate.
I hate that everyone has an opinion.
I hate that you agree with so many of the things I hate.

I hate that when everyone finds out I wrote this book, they will tell me the things they hate too.
I hate negative people.
I hate having so much hate built up.

And finally . . .

In case you were wondering,
"Does this person like *anything*?"
The answer is yes, I do.
Two things, actually.

1. I like that you bought this book, which means that I'm not alone on the things I hate.

2. I like puppies . . . but . . .

I hate happy endings.

So Much More to Hate . . .

P.S. . . . . I hate postscripts.

But, if you're optimistic . . . just like me, and you're craving for more loathing, then proudly join many people like you to keep the hates coming, or share some "hates" of your own at:

www.Thehatepage.com
Twitter: WhatIHateToday
Facebook: I HATE EVERYTHING

I hate that I had to write *www.* for those two people who still don't know how to enter a website address.

I hate that I'm addicted to social media sites.
I hate that it's the only way that I know how to be social.

Acknowledgments

I hate that I've gone on this long without acknowledging
the people who immediately supported the need to bring
this cynical commiseration to life. Thanks to Adams Media,
particularly the talented Brendan O'Neill, who creatively
loves to hate with us. And to my superagent, Taryn Fagerness
of the Taryn Fagerness Agency, who believed in my same
vision from the moment we met.

And to my supportive family, Mom, Dad, Marc, and Michelle;
along with Jen, my girlfriend; Klara and all my friends,
extended family, coworkers, neighbors, and to my puppy dogs
Chewie and Madalynn—I'd like to say, you have all been a
form of inspiration in one way or another; I assure you, it was
only positive.

I hate that you might not believe me.
I hate stretching the truth.
I hate that there isn't enough room to write out all of your names.

Who Is This Author Who Hates Everything?

Matthew DiBenedetti is an equal-opportunity hater. After working in the advertising industry for over twenty years, how could he not be? Matthew has worked on corporate marketing campaigns for everything from major sporting good brands and financial institutions to bookstore chains and fine china. He resides in Trenton, New Jersey, but loves to hate things worldwide.

I hate pen names.
I hate when good things come to an end.

DAILY BENDER

Want Some More?

Hit up our humor blog, The Daily Bender, to get your fill of all things funny—be it subversive, odd, offbeat, or just plain mean. The Bender editors are there to get you through the day and on your way to happy hour. Whether we're linking to the latest video that made us laugh or calling out (or bullshit on) whatever's happening, we've got what you need for a good laugh.

If you like our book, you'll love our blog. (And if you hated it, man up and tell us why.) Visit The Daily Bender for a shot of humor that'll serve you until the bartender can.

VISIT THE DAILY BENDER BLOG TODAY AT
www.adamsmedia.com/blog/humor